Azure Pipelines

Master Automated Deployment in Modern Web Applications

Table of Contents

Chapter 1. Introduction

In the digital realm of cut-throat competition, mastery over efficient tools propels one's ability to prosper. Welcome to our meticulously curated Special Report: "Azure Pipelines: Master Automated Deployment in Modern Web Applications". This report delves into the depths of Azure Pipelines, a key component of DevOps tools that redefines automated deployment in modern web applications. With burgeoning technologies, understanding complex concepts can become overwhelming. But worry not! This report is tailored for tech professionals of all levels, delivering an easy-to-comprehend guide to help you conquer the Azure Pipelines landscape. Whether you're an experienced developer looking to enhance your skillset or a novice in the world of web applications, this Special Report is designed to simplify the complexities and pave the path for your advancement. Embark on this journey of continuous integration and continuous deployment and leverage the power of Azure Pipelines to fuel your future!

Chapter 2. Introduction to Azure Pipelines

Azure Pipelines, a key service offered as part of Microsoft's Azure DevOps suite, transforms how we manage the lifecycle of our applications, especially in a dynamic and distributed environment. It is a platform that integrates developer tools for better collaborative software development. Let's unravel this tool and understand how it can optimize the deployment pipeline, starting from code integration to delivering a high-quality product to your end-users.

2.1. Major Components and their Functions

Azure Pipelines primarily consists of two integral components: Continuous Integration (CI) and Continuous Deployment/Continuous Delivery (CD). Continuous Integration is a mechanism where developers merge their changes back to the main branch as often as possible.

On the other hand, Continuous Deployment is the ability to get changes of all types—including new features, configuration changes, bug fixes, and experiments—through to production or into the hands of users, safely and quickly in a sustainable way.

These components work together to form a comprehensive software development pipeline, enabling developers to commit changes frequently, triggering automated builds and tests, ensuring that the application is always in a releasable state.

2.2. CI/CD Pipelines in Detail

CI/CD Pipelines are revered as the backbone of modern DevOps operations. They unite development and operations in a unified platform thereby eliminating manual intervention to a considerable extent.

Continuous Integration: Developers merge changes frequently, resulting in multiple daily integrations. Every check-in is automatically tested, ensuring detection of integration bugs early and significantly reducing the backlog. This process establishes a consistent and automated way to build, package, and test applications, improving team productivity and efficiency, while the application maintains a releasable quality.

Continuous Deployment: Although often used interchangeably, Continuous Deployment implies that every change goes through the pipeline and is automatically deployed to production, resulting in multiple production deployments every day. It ensures pushed updates or changes are correct and do not disrupt operations while allowing teams to release new updates to customers quickly.

2.3. Setting Up Pipelines in Azure

Setting up pipelines in Azure can be done in multiple ways, either through Azure portal, Azure CLI (Command Line Interface), or Azure PowerShell. The setup process typically involves the following steps:

1. Creating an Azure DevOps Project

2. Connecting with Source Control

3. Configuring Pipeline

4. Reviewing and running the Pipeline

2.4. What makes Azure Pipelines Stand Out?

Azure Pipelines scores high on versatility and compatibility fronts. It supports most of the known languages like Python, Java, JavaScript, PHP, C#, C++, Ruby, Go, Swift, and more, while also being container-friendly.

Among CI/CD tools, it offers the highest number of concurrent jobs with an ability to scale out as per requirements. It enables both cloud-hosted and self-hosted job hosting options, providing flexibility to organizations.

Moreover, its integration capabilities with a multitude of tools in the DevOps ecosystem, listening to Jenkins, Chef, Puppet, Red Hat, Ansible are remarkable and come with a promise of expanding the toolchain.

2.5. The Power of YAML

Azure Pipelines presents support for defining CI/CD Pipelines as code using YAML (Yet Another Markup Language). YAML pipelines align with the industry shift towards as-code methodologies and offer a plethora of benefits, including versioning support, enhancing audibility, supporting disposable environments, and reducing errors in the process.

This vast ecosystem of functionality warrants an in-depth exploration that we will undertake in the subsequent sections. By understanding Azure Pipelines, professionals can use this powerful tool to boost operational efficiency, expedite deployments, and ultimately deliver high-quality applications.

In the following chapters, we will delve deeper into each element of Azure Pipelines, discussing the architecture in detail, how to set up pipelines, how to configure a build and release, and even how the YAML paradigm works within Azure pipelines. This will provide a comprehensive understanding of Azure Pipelines, arming you with the knowledge to navigate this complex tool confidently.

In essence, Azure Pipelines embodies the ethos of DevOps in its ability to unite teams, streamline operations, and foster a culture of continuous learning and improvement. By gaining proficiency in Azure Pipelines, tech-professionals can not only enhance their skill sets but also drive their organizations' digital transformation initiatives.

Chapter 3. Automated Deployment: Scaling Modern Web Applications

The dawn of the digital era has positioned automation as a linchpin for handling complex, repetitive tasks. This paves the way for efforts vested in innovation, creativity, and strategic tasks. A standout instance in this narrative that encapsulates the power of automation is Automated Deployment. In modern web applications, deployment can exponentially scale the capabilities and streamline processes.

3.1. The Paradigm of Automated Deployment

Automated Deployment represents the practice of using automated tools to deploy software. The process eliminates manual intervention, thereby improving consistency, reducing errors, and substantially accelerating deployment time. It's a significant part of continuous integration and continuous deployment (CI/CD), a methodology that allows developers to integrate their changes into a mainline code base multiple times a day.

The core idea behind automated deployment is simple: the faster and more frequently you deploy new code, the quicker you can iterate and deliver new features to your customers or stakeholders. This, paired with the implementation of a robust feedback loop, results in significantly reduced lead time and heightens a team's agility.

3.2. Utilizing Azure Pipelines for Automated Deployment

Azure Pipelines is an indispensable tool in the realm of automated deployments. By supporting all popular programming languages and platforms, Azure Pipelines positions itself as a versatile solution that can work in almost any environment. The service supports two parts of the CI/CD development practice: Continuous Integration and Continuous Deployment. In the case of web applications, it offers a mechanism to automatically deploy your application to various stages of your deployment process.

Azure Pipelines work on the principle of pipeline-as-code, where you define your build and release process in a YAML file. This eases the process of replicating pipelines, reverting changes, and reviewing the history of pipeline adjustments in a version control system.

```
# Sample YAML file

trigger:
- master

pool:
  vmImage: 'ubuntu-latest'

steps:
- script: echo Hello, world!
  displayName: 'Run a one-line script'
```

The above example demonstrates a simple YAML file for an Azure Pipeline. When a change is detected on the master branch, the pipeline triggers and performs the scripted tasks on a virtual machine with the latest Ubuntu image.

3.3. Power of Parallel Execution

A significant feature provided by Azure Pipelines is parallel execution. It involves running multiple jobs simultaneously, which significantly reduces the time required to complete processes. It propels the trajectory of automated deployment, making it exponentially quicker. Moreover, it provides an opportunity for modern web applications to manage voluminous tasks without compromising on speed and efficiency.

3.4. Automated Testing: A Key Component

In the universe of continuous deployment, automated testing is a pivotal factor that perfectly complements automated deployment. Integrating automated tests in your azure pipelines can save time, ensure that no code changes are breaking the existing functionality, and help developers identify and rectify bugs faster. You can define your testing commands in the pipeline's script section to run tests.

```
# Sample YAML file with testing

trigger:
- master

pool:
  vmImage: 'ubuntu-latest'

steps:
- script: make test
  displayName: 'Run tests'
```

The above sample Azure Pipelines YAML file showcases automated testing. The 'make test' script runs all test cases, ensuring that the newly integrated code is robust, and does not break the existing functionality.

3.5. Deployment Strategies with Azure Pipelines

There are several deployment strategies that Azure Pipelines supports, each suited for different deployment scenarios.

Recreate: This strategy involves shutting down the existing version and then starting the new one. This strategy may involve application downtime, and hence is suitable for small, non-critical applications.

Rolling: The key idea is to gradually roll out the new version while taking down the old version simultaneously. This strategy ensures zero downtime, allowing continuous availability of the application services.

Blue/Green: In this strategy, two identical environments - blue and green - are maintained. One is live, say 'blue', while necessary adjustments and improvements are made in the 'green' environment. Once 'green' is ready, 'blue' is brought down, and 'green' goes live.

Canary Releases: Canary is a strategy that deploys a new version to a small subset of users before it rolls out to everyone. It helps in gaining feedback before a full-scale roll out.

Feature Toggle: A software delivery concept that toggles ON or OFF a particular functionality of an application. Useful for experimental features and aids in Continuous Deployment.

Each of these strategies offers a unique combination of risk management, speed, and versatility. An organization's choice among these strategies will largely depend on its specific requirements, level of risk tolerance, and deployment complexity.

In the world of modern web applications, automated deployment is no longer a luxury but a necessity. Azure Pipelines provides an excellent platform to harness the power of automated deployment. By understanding nuances and effective utilization, businesses can reap maximum benefits, from reduced error rates to significantly lower deployment times, thus ensuring continuous growth and innovation, scaled as per demand.

Chapter 4. Setting Up Your Azure Pipelines

In the digital realm, comprehending Azure Pipelines to the core entails an initial step of effective setup. This chapter is devoted to unravel the systematic process of setting up Azure Pipelines, an inevitable part of your DevOps toolkit.

4.1. The Prerequisites

To embark on this journey of mastering Azure Pipelines, it's crucial to have a few essentials in place. Here's a precise, comprehensive list:

1. A Microsoft Azure account. To explore Azure Pipelines or any service under Azure, having a Microsoft Azure account is mandatory. If you don't have one, head over to https://portal.azure.com and register for free.

2. Permissions to create a new project. You will require the necessary permissions to create a new project in the Azure DevOps organization.

3. Source code stored in a version control system. Azure Pipelines works with various version control systems such as Git, GitHub, and Azure Repos.

4. A basic understanding of Azure DevOps. This isn't exactly a prerequisite, but it comes in handy where you could encounter several DevOps buzzwords.

4.2. Project Creation In Azure DevOps

1. Log in to Azure DevOps from your Azure portal.

2. Click 'Create Project' at the top-right corner of the dashboard. A dialog box appears.

3. Enter the name and description for the project. Choose the visibility setting that suits your preference, either 'public' or 'private'.

4. Click 'Create' to initiate the creation process.

At this point, you'll have a brand new Azure DevOps project ready for Azure Pipelines configuration.

4.3. Configuring the Version Control System

Before entering into the depth of Azure Pipelines, it is critical to have your source code linked to a version control system. To perform this:

1. Navigate to the 'Repos' option in your Azure DevOps dashboard.

2. Azure offers the default option of initializing a new repository with a README, or you can import an existing repository.

Repeat the same procedure for all additional repositories your Azure Pipeline will deploy.

4.4. Setting Up Your First Pipeline

Now, let's focus on the creation of the first pipeline.

1. From your Azure DevOps project dashboard, go to 'Pipelines'.

2. Click 'New Pipeline'. The Azure Pipelines wizard will guide you to choose your code repository.

3. After selecting the repository, Azure Pipelines will present you with a number of defined pipeline templates. Choose the one that best fits your application. If none fit, opt for 'Empty Job'.

4. After selecting a template, you can define the steps that form your pipeline.

4.5. Defining Build Steps

Build steps are the tasks that the pipeline needs to complete. Examples of these tasks could be compiling code, running tests or creating deployable packages.

To create a new task:

1. From the pipeline's job, click '+'. A list of tasks will appear.

2. Search for the task corresponding to your needs.

3. Once found, click on 'Add'. The task parameters will appear.

4. Adjust the task parameters according to your requirements.

After these steps, your pipeline should be ready to be triggered either manually or by a pre-defined trigger, for example, a push to your Git repository.

4.6. Customizing Pipeline Triggers

Azure Pipelines provides flexibility to customize the triggers for your pipelines.

1. Locate your pipeline in the 'Pipelines' list and click 'Edit'. This will open the pipeline editing screen.

2. Click on the 'Triggers' option in the pipeline settings.

3. Use the 'Continuous Integration' option to set up your pipeline to run on every commit to your repository.

4. Additionally, you can define specific branches that the pipeline should run on, exclude certain branches, and even specify paths that should trigger the pipeline.

5. Save your changes.

Azure Pipelines has now been configured to run automatically whenever changes are pushed to the specified branches in your repository.

4.7. Fine-Tuning with Variables and Secrets

When setting up your pipeline, it is often necessary to work with variables and secrets. Variables are excellent to use when you have to deal with multiple environments (dev, stage and prod), while secrets are meant for sensitive data that should be hidden, like API keys.

To add a secret:

1. From your project's main page, navigate to 'Pipelines' > 'Library'.

2. Click on '+ Secure variable'. A dialog will appear.

3. Enter the name and the value of the secure variable.

4. Mark the 'Keep this value secret' checkbox.

5. Afterwards, save your changes.

To refer to a secret in your pipeline, you need to add `$(<secret-name>)` in your pipeline's YAML.

By the end of this setup guide, you will have your Azure Pipeline running efficiently, adhering to your commands, and aligning with your requirements. Careful and accurate setup helps in reducing barriers in the continuous integration and delivery process that lies ahead in your DevOps journey. Next, we will elaborate on how to manage, execute, and tweak these pipelines to your advantage.

Remember, the ability to handle such tools with proficiency spells a significant difference in the performance and timelines of your web applications. Comprehending and executing this vast world of Azure Pipelines accelerates your stride in the rapidly expanding universe of technology.

Chapter 5. Under the Hood: Azure Pipelines Architecture

As we venture deeper into the intricacies of Azure Pipelines, a comprehensive understanding of its architecture forms the backbone of automation potential. This chapter explores the primary components and workings of Azure Pipelines, allowing users a holistic view of the system.

5.1. The Core Components

Azure Pipelines operates through a set of interconnected components, forming a cohesive system where each piece plays a unique role in the pipeline process. To master Azure Pipelines, familiarizing with these components is essential.

1. Pipeline: It is the heart of the system, responsible for defining the steps for automating workflows. The pipeline houses two types of processes – Continuous Integration (CI) and Continuous Delivery (CD). Essentially, it describes what, when, and how to execute.

2. Jobs and Stages: Each pipeline is a sequence of stages. A stage is a logical boundary in the pipeline and generally represents an environment, like Production, Staging, etc. Each stage encompasses jobs, which represent an execution boundary – an agent starts executing the script and ends it when the execution is over.

3. Tasks: Every job within the pipeline is further broken down into tasks. Tasks are the smallest unit of work and represent individual commands within the CI/CD pipeline. Azure Pipelines provide several built-in tasks, and users can also add tasks from the Azure DevOps marketplace.

4. Triggers: These are the event-driven parameters in the pipeline

that initiate the process in response to specific changes or updates. Triggers can be set against a variety of events like code commits, pull requests, etc.

5. Artifacts: They are the outcomes - the result of a pipeline run. Artifacts could be compiled code, libraries, serverless functions, container images, or even static websites.

6. Agents: Agents do the heavy lifting of running the defined tasks. They are host machines where the pipeline actually runs. Azure Pipelines provide Microsoft-hosted agents, but users can also use self-hosted agents.

5.2. Setting up Azure Pipelines

To set up Azure Pipelines, one must initialize the pipeline configuration file, also known as YAML (short for YAML Ain't Markup Language) file. This file lives with your application code in the source repository and defines the tasks that should be executed by the pipeline.

The neat feature about the Azure Pipelines is that it supports a wide range of repository types such as Azure Repos, GitHub, Bitbucket, SVN, etc. It provides native integration with these repositories, making it easy to set up the pipeline.

When the pipeline reacts to a trigger, it reads the YAML file and executes the tasks defined inside. These tasks can be anything, like running scripts, compiling code, performing tests, or deploying the artifacts. The pipeline will also manage dependencies between tasks, ensuring they happen in the correct sequence.

5.3. Managing Azure Pipeline

Managing Azure Pipelines involves monitoring its performance, reviewing results, resolving failures, and improving the pipeline for efficiency. Azure Pipelines caters to all these management tasks efficiently. It provides a rich set of features to scrutinize pipelines and draw insights from the data.

Azure Pipelines provides an intuitive user interface that provides real-time updates on the status of all the pipelines in the system. It highlights failure points, if any, along with logging detailed diagnostic data.

The pipeline logs are especially helpful when resolving failures. They expose the under-the-hood details of every task executed in the pipeline, such as its initiation, duration, completion, errors, and dependencies. By examining these logs, one can determine where and why the pipeline failed.

In conclusion, Azure Pipelines architecture embraces a component-based model where each component plays a unique role in the pipeline's operation. The comprehensible setup, coupled with robust management features makes Azure Pipelines an exceptional tool to master for creating efficient, automated deployment processes in modern web applications. As the technology landscape continues to grow more complex, leveraging tools like Azure Pipelines can pave the way for growth and efficiency in enterprise operations.

Chapter 6. Configuring Build Pipelines: An In-depth Guide

Before embarking on the journey of configuring Azure Pipelines, it's crucial to understand the underlying concepts that envelop it, beginning with a 'Pipeline'.

In Azure DevOps terminology, a Pipeline encapsulates the entire process, starting from checking the version-controlled source code to delivery of the final product. A Pipeline gets divided into different stages, jobs and steps. Our primary focus in this chapter will be the 'Build Pipeline', which compiles all of the code and runs tests to ensure everything is functioning as expected before moving to deployment.

6.1. Preparing source code for the build pipeline

Before diving into configuring the build pipeline, you need to be prepared with your source code. This code could either be in your local repository or in a version control system like GitHub, Bitbucket, or SVN. If it's in a local repository, you need to push it to an Azure repository or any other version control system supported by Azure to make it accessible for the build pipeline. Azure Pipeline integrates perfectly with several source control tools, making it a seamless experience to run builds every time there's a commit pushed to your repository.

6.2. Creating and navigating the pipeline

Start by logging into your Azure DevOps account. In the DevOps homepage, find and click the 'Pipelines' section in the navigation panel.

A click on 'New Pipeline' will welcome you with a series of configuration options referred to as your build pipeline's 'configuration steps'. Select the option aligning with where your codebase is stored (Azure Repos Git, GitHub, Subversion etc.).

Next, Azure Pipelines will access the selected repository and identify the appropriate build templates corresponding to the programming language used. For instance, if your application is coded in Node.js, Azure Pipelines will recommend Node.js templates. Select the one that best fits your needs subject to the project's layout.

6.3. Configuration of tasks for build pipeline

Following the template selection, Azure generates a YAML file to process your builds. YAML, an acronym for "YAML Ain't Markup Language", primarily handles human-readable data serialization. This file, azure-pipelines.yml, houses all necessary instructions for your build pipeline.

Let's break down a basic azure-pipelines.yml file snippet:

```yaml
trigger:
- master

pool:
  vmImage: 'ubuntu-latest'

steps:
- script: echo Hello, world!
  displayName: 'Run a one-line script'
```

The 'trigger' keyword ensures that the pipeline runs each time a commit gets pushed to the implicated branch, in this case, 'master'.

'Pool: vmImage' dictates the type of machine to use for the build.

The 'steps' part defines the actions carried out when running the build. This sample script merely echoes 'Hello, world!' but usually constitutes a series of actions involving build, test, or deployment scripts.

To add a new task, Click the '+' button next to 'Agent Job 1' and peruse the Tasks pane. Here, select the task you want to incorporate and configure its settings according to your specific project requirements.

6.4. Setting up triggers

While discussing the YAML syntax, we touched upon the 'trigger' keyword. It's instrumental in initiating builds automatically whenever there's a commit made to the specified branch. To manually set up triggers:

1. Click on 'Triggers' tab.

2. Click '+ New' under 'Continuous Integration'.

3. Select the type of trigger and the branch to watch for changes.

6.5. Managing Variables

Environment Variables in Azure Pipelines provide flexible ways to manage your configuration. They can be defined at the scope of the pipeline and can be made secret too. To set these up:

1. Click on the 'Variables' tab in the Pipeline Editor.

2. Click on '+ New' and then add the 'Name' and 'Value' for your variable.

Once these steps are out of the way, it is time to save and run the pipeline. Your build should trigger based on the settings defined in the pipeline configuration.

As your application grows and evolves, your configuration needs will change, and Azure Pipelines offers the flexibility necessary to customize the build pipeline to fit the specific needs of your projects. As you become more comfortable with Azure Pipelines, the tool can become an indispensable part of your CI/CD strategy, aiding you in delivering reliable and efficient applications.

Mastering Azure Pipelines doesn't have to be daunting – with the right mindset and knowledge, even a complex tool like this becomes an asset, propelling you forward in your tech journey. Forge on, fellow tech professionals, and harness the power of Azure Pipelines to script your success!

Chapter 7. Efficient Handlings of Testing in Azure Pipelines

In the cycle of software development, testing is a crucial element that ensures the reliable operation of the application. Azure Pipelines, with its comprehensive suite for continuous integration and continuous deployment, provides an ideal environment for automated testing. Conveniently, Azure Pipelines supports a multitude of testing frameworks and languages.

7.1. Understanding Azure Pipelines and Testing

Azure Pipelines adopt a versatile approach for testing. It supports a multitude of testing tools and framework like JUnit, xUnit, NUnit, and others, facilitating both manual and automated testing. Leveraging these testing frameworks, you can design effective test cases for components ranging from individual functions to large, integrated systems.

One of the significant advantages Azure Pipelines offer is the parallel execution of tests. The Pipelines infrastructure allows for simultaneous testing across multiple environments, leading to an accelerated testing process. Furthermore, Azure Pipelines integrates not only with Visual Studio Test but also with third-party test suites, boosting its testing capabilities.

7.2. Configuring Testing Tasks in Azure Pipelines

The central focus when configuring tests in Azure Pipelines is the YML file. Here is a fundamental template to configure tests:

```
steps:
- task: Npm@1
  inputs:
    command: 'install'
- script: 'npm test'
```

The above pipeline denotes that Npm (Node Package Manager) installs all defined dependencies. The `npm test` command runs the tests. The location of the tests, the testing framework used, and the specific tests to be run are determined by the settings in the package.json file.

7.3. Integrating Test Suites

In cases where projects use test suites like Jest or Mocha for JavaScript, or NUnit for .NET, or JUnit for Java, the configuration of Azure Pipeline will vary. The setup in such scenarios needs you to specify the proper command to run the tests.

Here's an example configuration for running using Jest:

```
steps:
- task: Npm@1
  inputs:
    command: 'install'
- script: 'npm run jest'
```

The 'npm run jest' refers to a script specified in the package.json file. It considers test parameters and configurations defined there.

7.4. Test Reporting and Tracking

Azure Pipelines facilitate in-depth tracking and reporting for your tests. You can view test results in the Tests tab on the Pipelines page of Azure DevOps. Azure Pipelines creates an illustrative report displaying successful tests, failed tests, and current trends.

For a richer experience, Azure Pipelines allows for the integration of popular reporting tools, like Allure and ReportGenerator. The integration can provide you with granular reports and trending analysis, enabling you to spot and tackle code quality issues effectively.

7.5. Managing Parallel Testing

Azure Pipelines supports concurrent testing across multiple environments. This feature significantly reduces the testing time while ensuring exhaustive testing.

You can specify the maximum number of parallel jobs to run using the `jobs` flag in pipelines. If you need to test in different environments or configurations, use matrices of possible combinations. This matrix helps to streamline the testing process and helps to avoid potential bugs due to environmental differences.

7.6. Achieving Continuous Testing

Continuous Testing, an essential component of DevOps, involves a constant cycle of testing throughout the software lifecycle. With automated pipelines, tests are run at every step - from integration to deployment - ensuring that new features or changes do not disrupt existing functionality.

To achieve continuous testing, set up automated testing at different stages of your pipeline and ensure that the tests are exhaustive enough to catch issues early. Remember, the primary goal is quality assurance at every step.

In conclusion, Azure Pipelines equips you with robust tools for implementing exhaustive and effective automated testing. The ability to integrate with a multitude of testing frameworks, configure custom testing tasks, run tests in parallel, and deep dive into test results allows for a streamlined and thorough testing process, ensuring your application is robust and reliable. Embrace Azure Pipelines, equip your application with a formidable line of defense against bugs, and propel your success in the digital realm!

Chapter 8. Mastering Continuous Integration with Azure

Continuous Integration, or CI, is an important practice in modern software development, which involves integrating code changes from multiple developers into a central repository frequently. It allows for rapid detection and correction of errors.

When employed with Azure Pipelines, it leads to efficient and streamlined workflows. Azure Pipelines is an incredible DevOps tool that comes with fully cloud-hosted pipeline options, offering superb compatibility with several platforms and languages. Let's dive deep to comprehend the nitty gritty involved in mastering Continuous Integration with Azure.

8.1. Understanding Continuous Integration

Continuous Integration (CI) is a development practice where developers integrate code into a shared repository regularly. This approach significantly minimizes the integration problems and allows dev teams to develop cohesive software more rapidly. Most teams, for continuous integration, integrate their changes frequently - at least once a day or even several times a day.

Each integration can then be validated by an automated build and automated tests to promptly catch and report any integration errors as quickly as possible. In a nutshell, continuous integration embodies two critical practices: automating the build and test process, and integrating changes early and often.

8.2. Why Continuous Integration Matters

Several reasons contribute to the ever-increasing adoption of Continuous Integration (CI) process in software development. Firstly, early detection of errors, along with their wherewithal, noticeably quickens the development process. Secondly, integration bugs are detected and addressed quickly, minimizing the time spent tracking them down. Thirdly, there is no lengthy and tense integration period, making for a more pleasant development experience.

CI facilitates less backtracking to discover what went wrong, so developers can spend more time building new features. Automated deployment saves developers' time, and CI essentially gives development control back to the engineers.

8.3. Getting Started with Azure Pipelines

Azure Pipelines provide a versatile Continuous Integration/Continuous Delivery platform that can be used with virtually any language and platform. It supports building, testing, and deploying of your code. You can use Azure Pipelines to build workflows for both open-source projects and full-time enterprises.

To kick off the process, you'll need an Azure DevOps account. Then, create your new pipeline using the visual designer in the Azure DevOps portal.

8.4. Setting Up a Repository

Repositories act as storage for your code. You can use any Git repository with Azure pipelines. This could be on GitHub, Azure

Repos, or other Git repositories.

Start by generating a Git repository, and then connect it to your Azure Pipeline. Once linked, any code changes made in the repository will initiate the setup pipeline's build process.

After setting up the repository, define build triggers to initiate the pipeline whenever changes are pushed to your repository. Build validations allow you to fail a build if a check fails, ensuring issues are spotted before the build is even started.

8.5. Scripting Build Pipelines

The Build Pipeline is scripted using an azure-pipelines.yml file that sits in the root directory of your repository. This YAML file specifies the steps taken by the build, ranging from compiling the code to running the unit tests. You can customize the build process using this file.

For instance, a basic build pipeline script might look something like this:

```
trigger:
- master

pool:
  vmImage: 'ubuntu-latest'

steps:
- script: echo Hello, world!
  displayName: 'Run a one-line script'
```

This example shows a pipeline that is triggered whenever code is pushed to the master branch. When the pipeline runs, it uses an instance of the Ubuntu VM to execute a simple "Hello, World!" script.

8.6. Managing Artifacts

After a successful build, you need a way to store and manage the files created by the build process. These files, known as artifacts, can be anything from compiled code and build logs to test results.

The Publish Build Artifacts task is what you use to publish artifacts to Azure Pipelines or a Windows file share. These published artifacts are vital for distribution, deployments, and testing.

In conclusion, managing Continuous Integration with Azure isn't a daunting task if you've a clear understanding of its basic components and functionality. Wield the power of Azure Pipelines and deftly supercharge your automation capabilities to achieve faster, more agile software development.

8.7. Conclusion

Mastering Continuous Integration with Azure Pipelines can not only enhance your development process but also provide significant value to your overall project. It promotes a highly collaborative environment, continuously pushes for increased efficiency and, if implemented correctly, can remarkably reduce the time taken from development to deployment. The future of deploying modern web applications is automated, and Azure Pipelines is a vital tool in that future. Pioneering in its adaptation will surely hold you in good stead.

Chapter 9. Pushing the Boundaries: Continuous Deployment in Azure Pipelines

Awesome! Let's dive into the world of Azure Pipelines and continuous deployment.

Azure Pipelines is Microsoft's cloud-based continuous integration (CI) and continuous deployment (CD) service, which integrates well with various platforms and supports numerous languages. One of the most significant advantages of Azure Pipelines is its ability to deploy codes on various platforms, including hybrid environments, cloud, and legacy systems.

9.1. Understanding Continuous Deployment

Continuous Deployment is an approach in the software development practice where every code change goes through the entire pipeline and is automatically deployed to the production environment, making changes visible to the users instantly. The primary goal is to develop and deploy software quickly, reliably, and automatically.

It's worth noting that Continuous Deployment is not synonymous with Continuous Delivery, even though they share some similarities. The main differentiation lies in the deployment stage – while Continuous Delivery readies your application for deployment whenever needed, Continuous Deployment, on the other hand, does not require human intervention and the changes are automatically deployed to production.

9.2. Setting Up Azure Pipelines for Continuous Deployment

To leverage the continuous deployment with Azure Pipelines, you first need an Azure DevOps account. Once you have an account, create a new project and select 'Pipelines' on the left panel, then 'New pipeline'.

1. Connect your Source Control System (SCS): You can choose from GitHub, Bitbucket, or Azure Repos.

2. Specify the repository: After selecting the SCS, specify the repository where the codebase exists.

3. Configure the pipeline: Azure Pipelines offer both YAML and Classic Editor for pipeline setup. We recommend using YAML as it's more flexible and offers version controlling.

Here is a simple example of a YAML script for a Node.js application:

```yaml
trigger:
- main

pool:
  vmImage: 'ubuntu-latest'

steps:
- task: NodeTool@0
  inputs:
    versionSpec: '10.x'
  displayName: 'Install Node.js'

- script: |
    npm install
    npm run build
```

```
    displayName: 'npm install and build'
```

This script includes steps for getting the latest version of Node.js and runs 'npm install' and 'npm run build'.

1. Run the pipeline: Click 'Run' to execute the pipeline. You'll see the status and log of the run in real-time.

9.3. Implementing Continuous Deployment

After setting up your pipeline, the next step is implementing continuous deployment. For this, you need to define a deployment script in the pipeline.

In your YAML script, include 'Environments' and 'Deployment Jobs'. 'Environments' can define multiple stages of deployment like testing, staging, and production.

This script extends the previous one by adding a 'Deployment Job' to deploy a Node.js app to Azure App Service:

```
#previous code here

- stage: Deploy
  displayName: 'Deploy to Azure'
  jobs:
  - deployment: DeployWeb
    displayName: 'Deploy Web App'
    environment: 'Production'
    strategy:
      runOnce:
        deploy:
          steps:
```

```yaml
    - task: AzureRmWebAppDeployment@4
      inputs:
        ConnectionType: 'AzureRM'
        azureSubscription: '(Azure service
connection name)'
        appType: 'webApp'
        WebAppName: '(Name of the web app)'
        packageForLinux:
'$(Build.ArtifactStagingDirectory)/**/*.zip'
        enableCustomDeployment: true
        DeploymentType: 'webDeploy'
```

In this script, we have added a 'Deploy' stage that includes a 'DeployWeb' job under an environment named 'Production'.

The critical step here is the 'AzureRmWebAppDeployment@4' task. This is a deployment task provided by Azure to deploy an app to Azure App Service.

Remember to replace '(Azure service connection name)' and '(Name of the web app)' with the details of your Azure subscription and web application.

9.4. Continuous Deployment Best Practices

Continuous deployment indeed promises faster code deployment, better code quality, and quicker feedback. However, without a well-structured approach, it may lead to potential issues. Thus, implementing the following best practices can help ensure a seamless and efficient process:

1. Review and Audit: Regularly review your deployment scripts and processes, don't let complacency creep into your CD practice.

2. Test Everything: Test automation is crucial. Ensure extensive testing to minimize the chances of introducing bugs into the production environment.

3. Staged Rollouts: Instead of deploying changes to all users at once, consider rolling out in stages. This approach helps detect problems early.

Azure Pipelines provides a strong foundation to implement and manage your CI/CD practices. The ability to build, test, and deploy on any platform and cloud is a powerful tool in today's diverse world of software development.

Continuous Deployment via Azure Pipelines enhances your delivery practices, making your applications more robust and reliable, while enabling your teams to respond more swiftly to changes and feedback. Embrace the power of Azure Pipelines and let automation simplify your delivery process, thus pushing the boundaries of what your coding crew can achieve.

Chapter 10. Troubleshooting Common Azure Pipelines Issues

Azure Pipelines, a vital element of the Azure DevOps suite, enables developers to deploy applications with a high level of automation and efficiency. However, as with any complex system, issues can arise. Fear not! This chapter promises an exhaustive guide to aid you in troubleshooting frequently encountered problems with Azure Pipelines to keep your delivery pipeline flowing smoothly.

10.1. Identifying Failures in the Pipeline

When your pipeline fails, it's time to roll up your sleeves and start debugging. Azure Pipelines displays an error message whenever a failure occurs. The very first step, therefore, is to scrutinize the error log.

Error logs can provide crucial information regarding the type and point of failure, such as an issue with the source code, a test failure, or a deployment glitch. Ensure to dig deeper until you identify the root cause of the problem—only then can you successfully troubleshoot and move forward.

10.2. Dealing With Authentication Errors

Authentication errors are common, but luckily, they can be resolved relatively easily. Here are some possible actions:

1. Check whether the access token has expired. Regenerate it, if necessary.

2. Verify whether the proper permissions have been set for the pipeline to access resources.

3. Always verify your credentials, and be cautious about multi-factor authentication parameters.

10.3. Mitigating Issues Related to Code Quality

The elasticity of Azure Pipelines is a blessing that comes bundled with its own drawbacks. While the tool seamlessly integrates with a vast array of services, it may have trouble processing code that doesn't meet industry standards.

To counteract this, ensure to write clean, readable, and well-documented code. Make good use of the linting tools available for your specific language. Consider setting up a Code Quality Gate, consisting of specific rules that the code must meet, as part of your pipeline.

10.4. Overcome Agent-Based Pipeline Failures

Azure DevOps pipelines offer a choice between Microsoft-hosted and Self-hosted agents. While the former is more convenient, some specific tasks or circumstances may dictate the necessity of a self-hosted agent. Make sure to verify:

1. The agent is online and properly connected to Azure DevOps.

2. The necessary software is installed on the agent.

3. You have the appropriate permissions.

10.5. Squashing Test Failures

Automated tests are a fundamental part of a CI/CD workflow. If your tests fail, follow these steps:

1. Review test logs, analyzing what appears to have failed.

2. Run the problematic tests locally to reproduce the issue.

3. If a test is faulty, rectify it. If not, correct the pipeline.

10.6. Coping With Configuration Errors

While setting up your Azure Pipeline, you're likely to encounter configuration blunders. These may range from syntax errors in your YAML file to incorrect initialization of variables. To remedy these issues:

1. Validate your YAML's syntax.

2. Make sure to initialize variables before they're used.

3. Validate that the environment and deployment settings are correct.

10.7. Dealing With External Service Failures

DevOps Pipelines often coordinate multiple external services, such as Kubernetes, Docker, or a cloud platform. Issues may crop up with these services that impact your pipeline. When this happens:

1. Check the service's status page.

2. Research relevant logs from the service itself.

3. Attempt manual interaction with the service to understand the issue.

Remember, patience and persistence are key. Troubleshooting is more of an art than a science. As you grapple with each problem and learn to handle it effectively, your grip on Azure Pipelines strengthens, elevating you to mastery over this efficient tool. The golden rule? Never fear failure—embrace it, study it, and use it as a stepping stone to further your understanding and capabilities.

Chapter 11. Future Prospects: Azure Pipelines in Next-Gen Web Applications

Modern web applications have been spawning into an untamed digital landscape at an unparalleled pace. Their scale and complexity are continually intensifying, and in the face of this challenge, Azure Pipelines, a service of Azure DevOps, provides a versatile and mighty engine for the automation of deployment.

Azure Pipelines promotes the ardent ideologies of continuous integration (CI) and continuous delivery (CD) that form the backbone of today's web applications' development and deployment strategies. In the upcoming sections, we explore the future prospects of Azure Pipelines and its profound implications on next-gen web applications.

11.1. Automation and Integration with Emerging Technologies

As we envision futuristic web applications, we can expect further advancements in automation, courtesy of Azure Pipelines. In conjunction with technologies like artificial intelligence (AI) and machine learning (ML), Azure Pipelines could potentially empower developers with predictive analytics, accelerating deployment cycles and minimising error rates.

Specifically, AI and ML can help ascertain the optimal time for the initiation of CI/CD processes, scrutinise code vulnerabilities, forecast potential system outages, and monitor user behaviour to tailor superior user experiences. Picturing this synergy, Azure Pipelines' capacity for automation seems destined to extend well beyond traditional realms.

11.2. Robust Security Mechanisms

With the surge in cyber threats, security in web application deployment is a pressing concern. Azure Pipelines, built on Microsoft Azure's robust security framework, ensures secure deployments and maintains a high standard of compliance. In the future, we can anticipate more sophisticated security protocols built into Azure Pipelines, such as advanced threat detection and auto-remediation processes, ensuring an even more secure environment for deployment.

11.3. Continuous Delivery and Serverless Architectures

Serverless architectures are quickly becoming popular due to their scalability, cost-effectiveness, and simplicity. Azure Pipelines aligns well with serverless, as it supports numerous environments and platforms. As serverless architectures continue to evolve, Azure Pipelines will likely incorporate more flexible and efficient deployment options, fortifying its nuanced deployment capabilities across varied infrastructural patterns.

11.4. Seamless Collaboration for Global Teams

The future of work is remote. Azure Pipelines is designed for collaboration, irrespective of the team's geographical disposition. As remote collaboration tools become more ingrained in our work culture, Azure Pipelines will continually invest in features that make integration with these tools more seamless, fostering productive interactions among dispersed development teams.

11.5. Role in the IoT Ecosystem

The Internet of Things (IoT) is expanding, with more devices interconnected than ever before. Azure Pipelines caters to the needs of IoT development, coping with increased device diversity, corresponding software complexity, and the need for frequent updates. As IoT grows further, Azure Pipelines will likely develop tailored solutions to cater to the specific needs of IoT deployments.

As we sail into the future, the prospects are promising. Azure Pipelines is all set to continue its trek as a leading automated deployment tool by broadening its capabilities, adapting to advancements, and meeting the ever-evolving expectations associated with next-gen web applications. The ensuing transformations within Azure Pipelines will redefine the standards for CI/CD models and shape the contours of future web development and deployment.